WESTERN NEW YORK

There's So Much To Love

Writing by Mark Donnelly, Ph.D.
Photography by Mark Donnelly & Friends

RPSS Publishing • Buffalo, New York
www.rpsspublishing.com

Text and design by Mark D. Donnelly, Ph.D.
Photography by Dr. Mark D. Donnelly, as well as many photos graciously contributed for this project
by several prominent local photographers who share his passion for this city

Perfect Bound: ISBN 978-1-956688-03-0

Second Edition - Printed in the United States of America

17 18 19 20 21 6 5 4 3 2
www.rpsspublishing.com

Table of Contents

On the Cover:
An aerial view of Erie Basin Marina looking toward downtown Buffalo © Photo by Mark Brice, Buffalo Aerial Pictures

Opposite:
The south portico of the Buffalo History Museum during the flowering of the cherry trees. The sculpture in the pediment carved by Charles N. Niehaus represents the forces of civilization.

ARTVOICE

There's so much to love

"To be anyone, or go anywhere, you need to know where you came from. And I love my Buffalo roots."

Tim Russert – Former moderator of NBC's Meet the Press/proud Buffalo native

Here in Western New York, it's hard to look around and not to be awestruck by our vast wealth of arts, heritage, and special character of place. This region is home to a mind-boggling array of beautiful parks and gardens, cultural activities, a vibrant waterfront, architectural treasures, and dozens of remarkable neighborhoods, each with a unique pulse, spirit, and personality.

A walk down the street is, in many cases, a walk through our rich history. And there is a sensory overload of fairs, festivals, galleries, concerts, sports, and other amazing activities for everyone to get their heads and hearts around.

Please visit these places, frolic in our spectacular four seasons, and fall deeply in love with our city and region over and over again.

Opposite: An aerial view of Elmwood Avenue heading south toward downtown Buffalo © Photo by Joe Cascio
Above from left to right: • Mural at General Mills Plant. Cheerios are the official cologne of downtown Buffalo • A flock of Flow-mingos at Hoyt Lake • Entrance to Buffalo and Erie County Botanical Gardens • Lion relaxing and catching some rays at the Buffalo Zoo

Blessed with Four Seasons

While Buffalo is famous for its snow, if you dig a little deeper you'll discover that our region enjoys four distinct seasons, each remarkable in its own right.

Here in Western New York, we have the privilege of enjoying four very spectacular seasons, each with a distinctive tone and character. Real estate professionals have an explanation for this – location, location, location.

Tucked in between two of the world's largest freshwater lakes, it's here that we grow the grapes that make our NY State wines so famous. It's also here that we maintain a full range of ways to frolic – in the sand, in the leaves, in the snow, and beside the tulips.

While our weather diversity may play havoc on your closet space by necessitating the storage of everything from flip flops to ugly sweaters, it never truly reaches the extremes of many other cities. We lack days that exceed 99 degrees, tornadoes, mudslides, hurricanes, dust storms, and tsunamis, so at the end of the day, we always know where our houses are. According to the National Weather Service data, we are far from being the snowiest, blowiest, or coldest American city. In fact, when even our worst weather disasters are finished, we get to play in them.

Opposite: Winter- Frolicking in the snow at an area ski resort • Spring - The Buffalo History Museum flanked by cherry blossoms • Visitors at Brian and Gordon's Bird Street floral sanctuary during Open Gardens • Fall Festival at the Great Pumpkin Farm in Clarence.

WATSON
ELEVATOR

Our Rich History

"History, by connecting us to our past and to our community, helps us to understand our present, and provides us lessons to guide us towards our future."

In Western New York, history has never been a spectator sport. The narrative of the Underground Railroad, Women's Rights, the Chautauqua Movement, the Niagara Movement, the Arts and Crafts Movement, the War of 1812, a presidential assassination, and the development of modern architecture were all forged, in no small part, right here in our own backyard.

Fortunes were made by the likes of William G. Fargo, founder of American Express and Wells Fargo. Jazz legends like Louis Armstrong jammed at our Colored Musicians Club. And American presidents lived, governed, died, and were buried here.

The city's position at the western terminus of the Erie Canal made us the "Gateway to the West" – the departure point for immigrants on their way to the heartland. Today this area has been newly revived at Canalside.

Buffalo was also a gateway for runaway slaves seeking freedom on the Underground Railroad, then later fertile ground for the Civil Rights Movement.

In short, in Western New York, it's all too easy to walk on the very same ground where history vastly changed the world.

Left to Right: Buffalo, N.Y. hosted the Pan-American Exposition, which highlighted the cultures and achievements of Western Hemisphere • Buffalo Niagara Heritage Village is a 35 acre museum campus featuring 11 historic buildings, historic gardens, and a 25000 square foot exhibit building. • The SS Canadiana was a passenger excursion steamer that primarily operated between Buffalo, New York and the Crystal Beach Park in Crystal Beach, Ontario from 1910 to 1956. • The Buffalo Harbor Museum displays and exhibits provide an overview of the evolution of the Buffalo Waterfront along with artifacts from the vessels that sailed the Great Lakes.

Opposite: A pen and ink map of downtown Buffalo and its waterfront.

WAR OF 1812 | OLD FORT NIAGARA

The War of 1812 is a poignant reminder that war can happen as close as your backyard. Much of that fighting occurred right along the U.S. and Canadian border.

Old Fort Niagara, located at the mouth of the Niagara River, controlled access to the Great Lakes and the westward route to the heartland of the continent. Its history spans more than 300 years. The French established the first post here in 1679 and 1726. They erected a permanent fortification with the construction of the impressive "French Castle."

The fort was occupied by three nations: France, Great Britain, and the United States. Visited by nearly 200,000 people each year, this historic and scenic site will transport you back in time as costumed interpreters and - reveal the stories behind this legendary stronghold.

Opposite: The French Castle incorporated barracks space for soldiers, officers quarters, a trade room, chapel, storerooms, powder magazine, and bakery.
Left: The second-floor guard room in the French Castle.
Below: Reenactors simulating the Battle of Queenston

Erie Canal

The advent of the Erie Canal arguably made Buffalo the center of the known universe. It was the crossroads connecting the manufactured products from the east with the rich agricultural bounty of the west. The building of the Erie Canal became the principal driver behind Buffalo's explosive growth in the mid-to-late 19th and early 20th centuries.

In 1825, Buffalo became the focus of the most demanding engineering projects in the country. Built between 1817 and 1825, the original Erie Canal traversed 363 miles from Albany to Buffalo. Originally four feet deep and 40 feet wide, with removed soil piled on the downhill side to form a walkway known as a towpath. It cut through fields, forests, rocky cliffs, and swamps; crossed rivers on aqueducts; and overcame hills with 83 lift locks. Although its builders borrowed and adapted ideas and techniques from earlier European canals, they applied them with audacity on an unprecedented scale.

Despite the Canal Terminus's lofty role during its 1860s heyday, the waterfront was the polar opposite of paradise. Viewing it today, it's hard to imagine this area was formerly known as "the Infected District", a hotbed for drunkenness and debauchery, especially among visiting sailors. At one count, there were 75 "houses of ill-fame" and over a hundred saloons, all within an eighth of a mile radius.

After years of a remarkable transformation, Canalside is again the ground zero of Buffalo's renaissance and is a growing regional destination and entertainment district.

Left: On October 26th, 1825, the Erie Canal was officially completed. With much pomp and fanfare, Governor Dewitt Clinton made the ten day journey down the canal, from Buffalo to New York Harbor. At the harbor, Clinton ceremoniously poured Lake Erie water into New York Harbor, officially "Wedding the Waters." In a less elaborate ceremony two days later, Judge Samuel Wilkeson poured the briny ocean water into Buffalo's harbor, completing the Wedding of the Waters.

Opposite: Through the magic of Photoshop, a typical canalboat bringing goods from the East has been transplanted into a photo of today's rewatered Commercial Slip

FREEDOM CROSSING

The Underground Railroad was a secret network for those escaping slavery run by people who assisted by providing money, food, clothing, and temporary shelter. Many fugitive slaves came through Western New York, crossing to freedom in Canada using the Suspension Bridge in Niagara Falls and the Niagara River at Broderick Park.

Left: The Niagara Falls Underground Railroad Heritage Center celebrates, interprets, and preserves an unparalleled density of historic resources, narratives, sites, and experiences associated with the City of Niagara Falls.

Below: The Michigan Street Baptist Church, erected in 1845, was a legendary Underground Railroad station. The building provided refuge for hundreds of freedom seekers before they crossed the border to Canada. Later, the church became a meeting place for abolitionists and anti-lynching activists like Frederick Douglass, William Wells Brown, W.E.B. Du Bois, and Booker T. Washington, each of whom graced its sanctuary.

Opposite: The "Freedom Crossing" monument in Lewiston by Susan Geissler depicts a slave mother, father, and child ready to be taken across the river in a rowboat by Amos Tryon, a volunteer "Station Master."

Grain Elevators

Buffalo's giant concrete castles serve as monuments to a bygone era when they filled the skyline and served as a symbol of our industrial stature as the largest trans-shipment point of grain in the world.

In 1842, Buffalo's Joseph Dart, formerly a hat merchant, designed the first grain elevator. It was a tall, wooden structure for grain storage that employed steam power and an ingenious elevating mechanism called a "marine leg" that streamlined the way grain was unloaded. This innovation not only had a profound impact on profitability and productivity; it radically changed the role of the working class and the city's trajectory.

Highly flammable grain dust caused fires that were the demise of the early wooden elevators. Over the next 50 years, the wooden elevators evolved into massive concrete structures up to a quarter of a mile long.

Grain elevators influenced the development of modern architecture, especially skyscrapers. While many are still in active use, the remainder has sat quietly at the water's edge for years, waiting for those with the imagination to put them to creative reuses. Their patience is now being rewarded with their recent transformations to art and performance spaces, recreation areas, and even a brewery.

Opposite: Fog rolling in along the grain elevators on the Buffalo River
Right: Scoopers who aid in loading and unloading the grain into the "leg," which draws grain into the elevator utilizing an endless belt of buckets.
Below: The Edward M. Cotter in Buffalo is the oldest active fireboat in the world and has been fighting fires caused by grain dust since 1900.

Roycroft Campus

The Roycroft Campus in East Aurora, NY, was home to a significant cultural movement that was a response to the mass production of the applied arts. Roycroft was a reformist community of craftworkers and artists founded in 1895 by Elbert Hubbard, which formed part of the Arts and Crafts movement. His championing of the Arts and Crafts approach attracted many visiting craftspeople to East Aurora and they formed a community of printers, furniture makers, metalsmiths, leather smiths, and bookbinders.

The Roycroft Campus is the best preserved and most complete complex of "guild" buildings remaining in the United States that evolved into centers of craftsmanship and philosophy. It was awarded National Historic Landmark status in 1986.

Opposite: The Copper Shop, constructed in 1902 in the style of a small English cottage, was used as a second blacksmith shop where they created hammered copper products and bottled East Aurora maple syrup and honey.

Right: A letterpress printing display at the Power House visitor center. Built in 1910 to furnish heat and electricity to the entire Campus through an underground piping system, the Power House was destroyed by fire in 1997 and rebuilt in 2012.

Below: Aphorisms abound at Roycroft Inn East Aurora New York .

Theodore Roosevelt Inaugural National Historic Site

The Wilcox Mansion, also known as the Theodore Roosevelt Inaugural National Historic Site is an early nineteenth-century Greek Revival mansion. Owned by the Ansley Wilcox family, it was here in the library that Teddy Roosevelt took the oath of office as our 26th President after the assassination of President William McKinley at the Pan-American Exposition. It is now a museum showcasing items related to both the assassination and the inauguration in 1901.

Opposite: The exterior of the Wilcox Mansion in a blanket of white during a truly unique Western New York holiday tradition – Victorian Christmas

Left: The Greek-Georgian Revival-style dining room where Theodore Roosevelt would have had his meals adds a humanizing touch to a very tumultuous moment in Buffalo's history.

Below: The library where Theodore Roosevelt took the oath of office.

NATIONAL PARK SERVICE
Theodore Roosevelt Inaugural
National Historic Site
↑ Visitor Center
"Today...I welcome you here...
we wish you well; we wish you
all prosperity and...we earnestly
hope for your well-being."
- Theodore Roosevelt, at the opening
of Buffalo's Pan-American Exposition
May 20, 1901

Buffalo Transportation Pierce-Arrow Museum

Pierce-Arrow was once one of the most recognized and respected names in the burgeoning automobile industry. For 38 years, the Buffalo-based Pierce-Arrow Motor Car Company produced some of the finest automobiles in the world, supplying cars to the White House for the use of the President for more than 20 years. In 1906, the company built a large automotive plant in Buffalo. After making what were arguably the best bicycles in the world, they turned their attention to high-end, luxury cars.

Right: You will find a selection of significant transportation items with an emphasis on Pierce-Arrow, the E.R. Thomas Motor Company, and other Buffalo-made automobiles and their accomplishments.

Opposite: In a 40,000-square foot glass-and-steel atrium stands the centerpiece of the museum–a filling station designed by famed architect Frank Lloyd Wright in 1927. It was proposed for the then intersection of Michigan Ave and Cherry Street, now covered by the Kensington Expressway, but was never built.

Below: Hood ornament from a 1930s Pierce Arrow

BUFFALO, N.Y.
1934
PIERCE-ARROW

Above: Piano:Dizzy Gillespie • Trumpet: Elvin Shepard • Sax:Wilbur Trammel • Miles Davis standing in the doorway • John Coltrane is also in the photo.

Colored Musicians Club

Up the narrow, steep stairway is where the magic happens. Upon entering The Buffalo Colored Musicians Club, you will be bathed in the echoes of a master class in jazz history. Through this same door has passed jazz legends such as Dizzy Gillespie, Count Basie, Art Blakey, Duke Ellington, Lionel Hampton, Billie Holiday, Ella Fitzgerald, and dozens of others.

Live jazz can still be heard in the upper room, which hasn't changed much over the decades. Members offer free jazz lessons to community youth and hold a jam session at the club on Sunday evenings.

Right: The Colored Musicians Club is the oldest running African-American club in the United States. It formed in 1918 and found its current home on Broadway in 1934. In 1999, it was designated a historical preservation site, and in 2018, it was designated as a National Historic Site.

Below: Currently, the Club is promoting historical research and the preservation of jazz in Buffalo. The first floor of the Colored Musicians Club is now a museum showing off its rich history.

Parks & Gardens

"A park is a work of art, designed to produce certain effects upon the minds of men."

–Frederick Law Olmsted

Buffalo's parks and gardens are a wealth of cultural gems that breathe life into virtually every neighborhood. They provide the serenity of grass and trees where you most need them and bursts of color where you least expect them. During the 1901 Pan-American Exposition, Buffalo was celebrated not only as the City of Light, but the City of Trees.

Distinguished for their creativity in designing New York City's Central Park and Brooklyn's Prospect Park, Frederick Law Olmsted and Calvert Vaux were called upon by the Buffalo Parks Commission in 1868 to design parks for Buffalo.

Their unique design included not one but three parks: The Park (Delaware Park), The Parade (Martin Luther King, Jr. Park), and The Front Park, complete with connecting parkways and circles. As Buffalo expanded, Olmsted and Vaux were again called upon to enlarge the park system by adding additional parks, including Riverside, Cazenovia Park, and South Park. While the 850 acres of this historic urban park system are stellar in their own right, today it only comprises less than 75% of the city's parkland used for recreation, relaxation, and rejuvenation.

Western New York has an insatiable celebration of all things green. This is evidenced by our Garden Walk, the Buffalo and Erie County Botanical Gardens, WNY Peace Gardens, Niagara Falls Great Lakes Garden, and virtually everywhere else a flower will fit.

Left to right: The War of 1812 Bicentennial Gardens celebrates the friendship between the USA and Canada for more than 200 years. • The lush gardens surrounding the Darwin Martin House. • Sunflowers Of Sanborn • Buffalo not only roam in our zoo, they also hang out at the Lasalle Park playground.
Opposite: Children beating the summer heat at the splash pad at Martin Luther King, Jr. Park

Cheeri-FLO

Delaware Park

One of Olmsted's first three parks in Buffalo, Delaware Park serves as the focal point of the Olmsted system and today contains or borders many of Buffalo's cultural institutions such as the Buffalo History Museum, Albright-Knox Art Gallery, Shakespeare in Delaware Park, and the Buffalo Zoo. Simply named "The Park" by Olmsted, these 350 acres of meadow, forest, and lake serve as Buffalo's version of "Central Park".

Hoyt Lake, the centerpiece of Delaware Park, is named in honor of William Ballard Hoyt II, a former member of the State Assembly whose vision, dedication, and concern for the environment helped beautify and preserve the lake for the people of Buffalo.

The Buffalo Olmsted Parks Conservancy has reintroduced rowboats on the lake, creating one of the most enjoyable ways to spend time in Delaware Park. The replica rowboats were designed and built by the Buffalo Maritime Center.

Opposite:
A new fleet of nine bright pink flamingo paddle boats is available for hourly rental through Hoyt Lake Rowboats.

Right:
One of the many unique places within The Olmsted Park System is the historic Rose Garden. Flanked by the Marcy Casino and atop Shakespeare Hill, the Rose Garden's blaze of beautiful flowers and its pergola has been a popular site for wedding photos since 1912.

The garden features many varieties from the All-America Rose selections planted in 33 different beds.

Forest Lawn Cemetery

Hiding in plain sight, right in the middle of the city, are 269 pastoral acres that define beauty and solitude. Founded in 1849, Forest Lawn is one of America's premier historic cemeteries and one of the world's finest outdoor museums.

Many of its monuments, sculptures, and mausoleums are designed by great sculptors and architects, including Stanford White, Augustus Saint-Gaudens, Harriet Frishmuth, E. B. Green, Richard Upjohn, and Frank Lloyd Wright.

In a tradition that began over 150 years ago, Forest Lawn remains a vital place where past and present are joined and visitors are warmly welcomed. Picnics, tours, and creative events are held there to enrich the life of the community. Such activities foster the ultimate tribute: Those departed are surrounded by vibrant life, ensuring that they are perpetually remembered.

Forest Lawn's great tradition of welcoming visitors grew out of a concept that originated at Père-Lachaise in 1805. This Parisian cemetery was the first to create a park-like space with bucolic vistas intended to attract the living. In addition, it encouraged families to visit and remember their loved ones. As a result, Forest Lawn became one of the first such cemeteries in America, inviting the public to enjoy its beauty and celebrate its residents.

Right: "The Three Graces" fountain sculpture by Buffalo-born Charles Cary Rumsey (1879-1922) is located on Mirror Lake.
Below: Blue Sky Mausoleum designed by Frank Lloyd Wright

Japanese Garden

The Japanese Garden represents a gentle, horticultural gesture of friendship between two sister cities: Buffalo, New York and Kanazawa, Japan. Located on six acres on the bank of Delaware Park's Mirror Lake, it originally began in 1974 with more than 1,000 plantings, 20 globe lights, and three small islands connected to the mainland by delicate bridges.

Gardens After Dark Series: The Botanical Gardens filled with colorful and soft lighting to enhance and showcase their plant collection

Buffalo and Erie County Botanical Gardens

A perfect respite from the daily grind, the Buffalo and Erie County Botanical Gardens is the best place in Buffalo to enjoy the beauty of exotic horticulture treasures from around the world. Open year-round, it's designed to be a living museum that inspires curiosity and connects people to the natural world. Inside the conservatory you get a perfect connection with plants because you are in their world, not the other way around.

Created from the visions of extraordinary people; David F. Day, Frederick Law Olmsted, John F. Cowell, Frederick A. Lord and William A. Burnham, this masterpiece opened in 1900. Lord & Burnham, premier designers of Victorian glass houses brought these visions to life with their unique design that was based upon the famous Crystal Palace in England.

The 1901 Pan-American Exposition in Buffalo helped to spur the success of the South Park Conservatory by providing trolley rides from downtown Buffalo to the conservatory. Tens of thousands of people visited the breathtaking conservatory and delighted in the exotic collection of plants .

In 1981 the South Park Conservatory was sold to Erie County, and its name was changed to the Buffalo and Erie County Botanical Gardens. In 1982 the Botanical Gardens was placed on the National Register of Historic Places and the New York State Register of Historic Places.

WELCOME
GardenWalk
Front
Back
Side

Flower Power

Garden tours in communities throughout Western New York now pack our summer calendars, delighting green thumbs from near and far.

Garden Walk Buffalo Niagara

Garden Walk Buffalo Niagara is one of Western New York's most anticipated summer happenings. From its humble beginnings in 1995 which included only 29 gardens, today it features more than 1000 gardens and is now the nation's largest private garden tour. During the last weekend in July, an estimated 65,000 garden lovers pick up their maps and walk amidst our city's beautiful flora at homes that sport the familiar yellow signs.

Gardens at Erie Basin Marina

The Gardens at the Erie Basin Marina are more than just an amazing explosion of floral color; it's a test garden for companies that hybridize flowers for the home gardener. Brimming with over 300 varieties of annuals gracing our waterfront, this is an important proving ground supported by many seed companies testing flowers in this climate and location.

"I love when visitors stop, ask questions, and share their passion about gardening. It's not an interruption. I start planting early in the spring. By the time people come down here, it's summer and 80 degrees."

– Stanley Swisher
Superintendent of Grounds - Erie Basin Marina

Right: The Gardens at Erie Basin Marina

Opposite: A crowd of both people and flowers line Summer Street during Garden Walk Buffalo Niagara

NIAGARA FALLS STATE PARK

Niagara Falls State Park, established on July 15, 1885, is the model from which all other state parks were created. America's oldest state park, Niagara Falls State Park's magical combination of water, cliff, and gravity has mesmerized multiple generations. Remaining faithful to the vision of park designers Fredrick Law Olmsted and Calvert Vaux, the historic Niagara Falls State Park remains an amazing natural respite. They believed that parks should be places of natural beauty where "the masses could be renewed"

Each year, millions of visitors come to view the millions of gallons of water roaring over Niagara Falls every minute – about 750,000 gallons each second!

Niagara Falls State Park provides unparalleled access to experience this wonder from every angle. You can stand within feet of the brink of the Falls at Prospect or Terrapin Point. View from a point jutting out over the

Left: A parade of colorful rain ponchos at the Cave of the Winds
Below: Spectators get an amazing view of thr Bridal Veil and American Falls from Luna Island.
Opposite: A winter view of the Horseshoe Falls from Terrapin Point.

Niagara Gorge from the Observation Deck at the Cave of the Winds. Feel the mist on your face as you climb the stairs midway up the Falls to the Eagle's Nest. Discover why they provided rain ponchos and water sandals at the Cave of the Winds Hurricane Deck as waterfalls thunder down from incredible heights. Or, sail into the belly of the beast as the Maid of the Mist as it fights its way through the churning rapids directly below the Horseshoe Falls.

From the warmth of summer to the blaze of fall leaves and finally the breathtaking frozen mounds in winter, Niagara Falls State Park is a visual delight in all seasons.

There is nothing quite like summer at Niagara Falls State Park in Niagara Falls, New York. With the sun on your face and the wind in your hair, you can soak in the memories along with the views aboard the iconic Maid of the Mist. You can also enjoy a thrilling walk on the Cave of the Winds and feel the rushing torrents of the Bridal Veil Falls.

Well-integrated alongside this inspiring wonder of the world is the solitude of a park is filled with nature to be discovered and scenic terrain to be explored. Changing leaves, long walks, and hiking trails galore conspire to make fall a stunning time to visit Niagara Falls, New York. Explore its scenic terrain and breathtaking views on foot. All routes are flat and accessible for beginners, with self-guided tours and professionally led outings offering many choices. You haven't experienced the Falls until you've seen them in all their snow-white frosted majesty — and there's no better place to catch a view than the park's Prospect Point. The Cave of the Winds is open year-round and is a must-see in all four seasons.

When the snow has melted, and spring arrives, Niagara Falls State Park reclaims its rightful place with more than 400 acres of lush landscape.

Above: A field of frozen mounds at the base of the American Falls

Right: The Falls are stunning by night, bathed in colorful lights, and spectacular when illuminated by nightly fireworks displays.

NO
STANDING
HERE TO
CORNER

Arts & Culture

"Quite frankly, we're spoiled rotten."

Buffalo Niagara's embarrassment of cultural wealth is difficult to hide. Humility takes a back seat in a region that can boast a world-class philharmonic orchestra, internationally acclaimed art galleries, and award-winning theater. We are home to a mind-boggling array of music, theater, and dance, housed in some of the most amazing venues ever built to experience them.

We can explore the vibrant colors of our regional palette with more than its fair share of great art and great art galleries. From the Albright-Knox Art Gallery, one of the finest collections of modern and contemporary art anywhere in the world, and permanent collections like the Burchfield Penney, Castellani, Anderson, and CEPA, to hundreds of small, local galleries and studios, ours is a bustling region of the arts.

We're blessed by sharing a backyard with the awe-inspiring Buffalo Philharmonic Orchestra, sizzling jazz at the Colored Musicians Club, Shakespeare in Delaware Park, an outstanding array of museums, the Chautauqua Institution, Artpark, Shea's Performing Arts Center, and dozens of professional theater companies.

The possibilities are virtually endless: Dig fossils. See how electricity is made. Get up close and personal with everything from dinosaurs and polar bears, to wooden horses and butterflies. Walk through history. Escape as a runaway slave to freedom and reenact historical battles.

It's hundreds of cultural experiences to get your hands on and mind around to recharge your creative batteries.

Left to Right: • Grffis Sculputure Park in East Otto, NY. Situated on over 400 acres, it has around 250 sculptures exhibited. • The Castellani Art Museum serves as a cultural resource for Niagara University • The NACC - Niagara Arts & Cultural Center • Mastodon skeleton at the Buffalo Museum of Science

Opposite: The Freedom Wall, 2017- on the corner of Michigan Avenue and East Ferry Street. Its part of The Albright-Knox Art Gallery Public Art Initiative.

The Buffalo Zoo

The Buffalo Zoo is a vibrant collection of wild and exotic animals and houses more than 320 species of plants. Founded in 1875, it's the third oldest zoo in the U.S. and is listed on the National Historic Register. Located on 23.5 acres of Buffalo's Delaware Park and open year-round, the zoo is a source of recreation, education, and conservation. Each year, the Buffalo Zoo welcomes approximately 400,000 visitors and is the second largest tourist attraction in Western New York; second only to Niagara Falls.

The Zoo's mission is to provide the general public with an educationally, culturally and recreationally significant community resource. This is accomplished through the advancement and encouragement of the science of zoology, through the conservation of the world's wildlife and through the innovative exhibition of diverse species of mammals, birds, reptiles, amphibians and fish.

Today, the philosophy of the Buffalo Zoo is to exhibit animals and plants in ecological habitats and geographical arrangements that represent the biomes of the world.

Rainforest Falls, a year-round zoo attraction, replicates the unique geology and ecology of Venezuela's Canaima National Park, home to Angel Falls, the highest waterfall in the world. In addition to showcasing a rich variety of wildlife, the back wall of the exhibit resembles a flat-topped mountain with a live, working waterfall.

At Sea Lion Cove, families get a commanding view of a group of charismatic, vocal sea lions. Visitors can view these large, graceful mammals from below the water as well from the 220-seat amphitheater.

The Arctic Edge focuses on the snowy, frozen climate of the Arctic Circle. Visitors get an up-close look at the bears' playful antics and enclosures that feature Arctic wolves, lynxes, and the majestic bald eagle.

Left:
A baby gorilla, as curious about its visitors as they are about him

Opposite:
Parents and children lining up to be amazed, amused, and much more aware of the world and the animals that fill it.

general
admission
buffalozoo
members

Albright-Knox Art Gallery

The Albright-Knox Art Gallery, one of the nation's oldest public arts organizations, is a world-class showplace for modern and contemporary art with a large selection of significant works by Gauguin, van Gogh, Picasso, Matisse, Pollock, and Warhol.

Visiting the Albright-Knox invites a reexamination of the old with the new in innovative and exciting ways. Their constantly changing installations and special exhibitions that pair contemporary art with the masterworks of modernism always promise unexpected surprises.

The Albright-Knox's legacy of visionary collection development, its artist-centric approach and ability to institutionally reinvent itself over time, is extraordinary.

–Janne Sirén, PhD
Director, Albright-Knox Art Gallery

Designed by the distinguished Buffalo architects E. B. Green and William Sydney Wicks, the building was originally intended to be used as the Fine Arts Pavilion for the Pan-American Exposition in 1901, but construction delays caused it to remain uncompleted until 1905, well after the end of the Exposition. The Albright-Knox Art Gallery can boast having 102 Ionic columns, second only to the U.S. Capitol.

AKAG has expanded its reach beyond their traditional walls. The Albright-Knox's Public Art Initiative integrates a wide range of artwork into publicly accessible spaces which are designed to enhance our shared sense of place and cultural identity in Western New York.

Opposite: Visitors marveling at "Monet and the Impressionist Revolution, 1860-1910," a limited spotlight presentation dedicated to Monet within a larger body of synchronous artists' works from the museum's Collection

Right: Caryatid on the east facade copied from the Greek Erectheum.

BUFFALO HISTORY MUSEUM

The Buffalo History Museum, formerly The Buffalo and Erie County Historical Society, collects and preserves the artifacts and records of Western New York. Founded in 1862, the Buffalo Historical Society's first president was Millard Fillmore.

The building, designed by Buffalo architect George Cary, is the only permanent structure erected for the Pan-American Exposition, which took place in 1901. It was designated a National Historic Landmark in 1987 and boasts more than 80,000 treasures.

On view by appointment in the Museum's Resource Center on Forest Avenue is the gun used by Leon F. Czolgosz to shoot President William McKinley at the Exposition's Temple of Music on September 6, 1901.

The building is an unaltered example of the work of the Beaux-Arts by Buffalo architect George Cary. He also designed the additions in 1927-29, maintaining the "aesthetic unity" of the building. In 1929 sculptural frieze panels by Edmond Amateis was added to the exterior to commemorate significant episodes in the history of the Niagara Frontier.

The museum was designated a National Historic Landmark in 1987 and boasts more than 80,000 historic treasures. It now hosts a number of regional history exhibits, including a recreation of Buffalo native and former Meet the Press host Tim Russert's office, as well as an archive of hundreds of thousands of documents and artifacts related to the history of the City of Buffalo and Erie County.

Opposite: The design of the beautiful south portico of the Buffalo and Erie County Historical Society, which overlooks Mirror Lake in Delaware Park, is a scaled-down version of the east front of the Parthenon in Athens, Greece.

Right: a recreation of Buffalo native and former Meet the Press host Tim Russert's office.

BUFFALO PHILHARMONIC ORCHESTRA

The Buffalo Philharmonic Orchestra is one of the brightest jewels in Western New York's long list of cultural treasures. Since its inception in 1938, the artistic excellence of the BPO has consistently enriched the quality of life in Western New York.

In fall and winter, the BPO performs at the orchestra's permanent home at Kleinhans Music Hall, a National Historic Site with an international reputation as one of the finest concert halls in the United States. And when the weather breaks, they become road warriors, mesmerizing crowds at dozens of diverse locations from Bison's games, Artpark, and Canalside, to the Shaw Festival and even Carnegie Hall.

As Buffalo's cultural ambassador, the Grammy Award-winning BPO, under the leadership of music director JoAnn Falletta, presents more than 120 Classics, Pops, and Youth Concerts each year and reaches over 40,000 students across all eight counties of Western New York.

Above:
The Buffalo Philharmonic Orchestra and Chorus in Kleinhans Music Hall
© Photo by Nickel City Studio

Right:
JoAnnFalletta conducting © Photo by Mark Dellas

"I've enjoyed every place I've conducted, but there's a rightness about this place. Yes, we can make good things happen here. We can play for a community we know and love. That is truly a collaborative relationship, and it's rare."

JoAnn Falletta
Music Director
Buffalo Philharmonic Orchestra

Burchfield Penney Art Center

The Burchfield Penney Art Center is a museum dedicated to the art and vision of Charles E. Burchfield and distinguished artists of Buffalo Niagara and Western New York. Through its affiliation with Buffalo State College, the museum encourages learning and celebrates our richly creative community.

In addition to its visual arts offerings, the Burchfield Penney has very diverse programming, regularly presenting concerts, literary readings, lectures, symposia, workshops, and special events.

Originally named the Charles E. Burchfield Center, the museum held its official opening ceremonies on December 9, 1966, with Burchfield himself in attendance. He died just a month and a day after the museum's inauguration. The museum maintains the world's most extensive collection of Burchfield's work and many other distinguished artists of Buffalo, Niagara, and Western New York.

The museum has since moved from its original space at Rockwell Hall to its new home across the street designed by Gwathmey Siegel & Associates Architects.

Today, one of the Burchfield Penney's main goals is to be unique and inviting to the public. Its "Front Yard" exhibit features three tall steel projectors which project constantly changing artwork onto the exterior of the building.

Left: The Elmwood Avenue face of The Burchfield Penney Art Center. *The familiar clock tower of Rockwell Hall at Buffalo State College is relfected in the windows.*

Opposite: The Center's main gallery

Chautauqua Institution

The Chautauqua Institution is a not-for-profit, 750-acre educational center beside Chautauqua Lake. It's a community of artists, educators, thinkers, faith leaders, and friends dedicated to exploring the best in humanity. For the approximately 7,500 persons in residence on any day during their nine-week season, and the over 100,000 who attend scheduled public events, it's a place where wisdom will be gleaned, memories will be made, and lives will be enriched.

Over 8,000 students enroll annually in the Chautauqua Summer Schools, which offer courses in art, music, dance, theater, writing skills, and a wide variety of special interests.

Chautauqua as a community celebrates, encourages, and studies the arts and treats them as integral to all of learning. With symphony, opera, theater, dance, visual arts, and a renowned music school, Chautauqua produces an "ecstatic mix" of programming that can be found nowhere else.

Self-improvement through lifelong learning was at the heart of the impulse that motivated Americans and founded Chautauqua in 1874. Today, that tradition continues with a morning and afternoon lecture platform, continuing education courses, the Chautauqua Literary & Scientific Circle book club, writers in residence, and a public library.

On the Boards

Over 250,000 patrons annually attend Sheas Performing Arts Center, a spectacularly restored European-style opera house designed by Cornelius and George Rapp in 1926. Listed on the National Registry of Historic Places, it is one of the only remaining Tiffany-designed theaters in the country. Originally an elaborate silent movie house, Sheas later became a place for live vaudeville shows with stars like the Marx Brothers, Bing Crosby, Frank Sinatra, Cab Calloway, George Burns, and Gracie Allen all having appeared on its elegant stage.

Today Sheas presents the broadest range of performing arts in the region, including touring Broadway musicals, concert artists, family shows, comedy, education programming, local school presentations, historic tours, special events, and a free family film series.

Left: A crowd gathers in front of the Sheas Performing Arts Center as the 600 block of Main Street floods with hundreds of theater-goers. It's part of "Curtain Up" the annual celebration of the opening of the Buffalo Theater Season.

Below: The opulence of Sheas as viewed from the stage.

On the Grass

Directly behind the lovely Delaware Park rose garden stands a grand Tudor-style stage on a sweeping hill of green. In this beautiful setting under the stars, Shakespeare's stories live on to explore the truths of the human heart: tragedy, jealousy, foolishness, passion, laughter, and love.

Shakespeare in Delaware Park is a Buffalo summer tradition. It was founded in 1976 as a summer apprenticeship program for theatre students from SUNY Buffalo to work alongside professional actors. The high-quality productions were so well received by the community that the program expanded and grew into the beloved professional theatre company and Western New York summer tradition that it is today. It is the country's second most successful outdoor Shakespeare festival in terms of audience, attracting an average of 50,000 patrons each summer. They are a not-for-profit, professional theater company dedicated to providing free, high-quality public theater to the widest possible audience.

"We believe in the emotive power of live theatre to enrich, inspire, and entertain our community. We started very modestly with one play and the audience response was terrific. Within a few years we were welcoming 50,000 people a summer. Now we play to about 2,000 people a night, with shows six nights a week."

– Saul Elkin, Founder and Artistic Director
Shakespeare in Delaware Park

Right: An audience, complete with wine, cheese, and a sea of blankets enjoying a captivating performance of Twelfth Night *on Shakespeare Hill.*

Architecture

Here in Western New York, we not only have the privilege of standing on the shoulders of giants – we also get to live in their houses.

Buffalo is literally a walkable encyclopedia of amazing architecture, told through the works of internationally renowned masters such as Frank Lloyd Wright; Louis Sullivan; H. H. Richardson; Daniel Burnham; McKim,Mead & White; Eliel and Eero Saarinen; and dozens of great local architects including E.B. Green and Louise Blanchard Bethune.

Buffalo also contains many buildings designed by modern architects, including Minoru Yamasaki, Toshiko Mori, Harrison & Abramovitz, and Mehrdad Yazdani of CannonDesign.

These masterworks are framed by the radial street plan designed by Joseph Ellicott and a series of parks and parkways implemented by Frederick Law Olmsted and his partner Calvert Vaux.

"Buffalo was founded on a rich tradition of architectural experimentation. The architects who worked here were among the first to break with European traditions to create an aesthetic of their own, rooted in American ideals about individualism, commerce, and social mobility."

–Nicolai Ourousoff
The New York Times

Left to right: One M&T Plaza was designed by Minoru Yamasaki and completed in 1966. If the design looks at all familiar, it's because Yamasaki also designed the former World Trade Center in New York City. • The Lombard-Romanesque style of Blessed Trinity RC Church • Frank Lloyd Wright's Fontana Boathouse • The French Renaissance-style Hotel Lafayette was designed principally by Louise Blanchard Bethune, this country's first professional woman architect. © Photo by Jackie Albarella

Opposite: Kleinhans Music Hall was designed in 1938 by Eliel & Eero Saarinen, the Michigan-based internationally famous Finnish architects. The concert hall, internationally renowned for its acoustic excellence, was originally built for and is currently home to the Buffalo Philharmonic Orchestra.

Frank Lloyd Wright's Darwin Martin Complex

The complex was designed by Wright, between 1902 and 1905, for businessman Darwin D. Martin, an executive at Larking Soap Company. While Wright was designing his famous Larkin Building, Martin had the occasion to appreciate Wright's work and commissioned him the design of a residential complex for his and his sister's families in Buffalo's Parkside neighborhood.

Built in his iconic Prairie style, the Martin House is a multi-residential estate. Wright's genius touched everything from the extensive interior and exterior gardens to the stained glass windows and furnishings. Three structures for Darwin Martin define the multi-residential estate, Martin's sister Delta Barton and the gardener. A 180-foot-long pergola links these dwellings to the conservatory and carriage house. Wright referred to this masterwork as his domestic symphony.

The Martin House is a prime example of a Prairie house, a revolutionary design developed by Frank Lloyd Wright. It's characterized by all the distinctive elements of the style, such as strongly marked horizontal lines, cruciform plans often featuring pergolas and verandas, hip roofs with large overhanging eaves, masonry and timber construction, a simple decoration, and strong integration of architecture and landscape.

Over the decades, the Martin House estate suffered considerable damage, and three of the original five buildings were demolished. In 1992, the Martin House Restoration Corporation (MHRC) was formed to raise funds and oversee a complete restoration of the estate. Extensive reconstruction efforts began in 1997, and the renovated property is now a world-renowned museum piece of Wright's work.

Right: Visitors are greeted with a dramatic 180-foot view from the Martin House front door down a walkway connected to a sunlit interior garden in the conservatory and a replica statue of the Nike of Samothrace.

Opposite: Darwin Martin House south façade

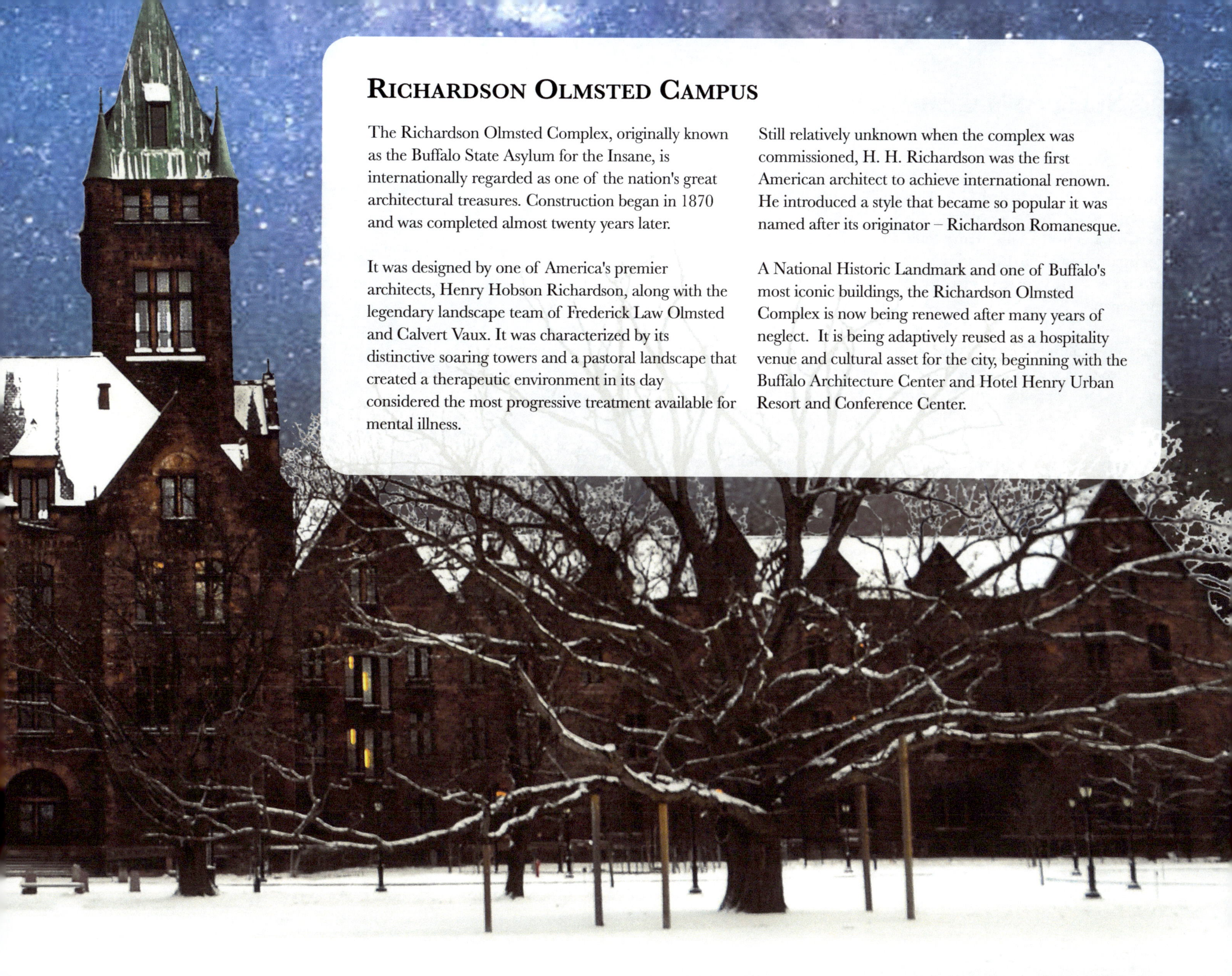

RICHARDSON OLMSTED CAMPUS

The Richardson Olmsted Complex, originally known as the Buffalo State Asylum for the Insane, is internationally regarded as one of the nation's great architectural treasures. Construction began in 1870 and was completed almost twenty years later.

It was designed by one of America's premier architects, Henry Hobson Richardson, along with the legendary landscape team of Frederick Law Olmsted and Calvert Vaux. It was characterized by its distinctive soaring towers and a pastoral landscape that created a therapeutic environment in its day considered the most progressive treatment available for mental illness.

Still relatively unknown when the complex was commissioned, H. H. Richardson was the first American architect to achieve international renown. He introduced a style that became so popular it was named after its originator – Richardson Romanesque.

A National Historic Landmark and one of Buffalo's most iconic buildings, the Richardson Olmsted Complex is now being renewed after many years of neglect. It is being adaptively reused as a hospitality venue and cultural asset for the city, beginning with the Buffalo Architecture Center and Hotel Henry Urban Resort and Conference Center.

Louis Sullivan's Guaranty Building

Standing at thirteen stories, the Prudential, also known as the Guaranty Building, was one of the first steel-supported buildings in the world and the archetype of the modern skyscraper. It was the tallest building in Buffalo when architect Louis Henry Sullivan and partner Dankmar Adler designed it in 1896. Louis Sullivan richly covered all of the exterior surfaces with ornate terra-cotta featuring stylized foliage and geometric shapes.

The Guaranty building is an example of multi-use construction designed with different zones reflecting different use plans; the ground level was designed for retail and restaurants, and the upper floors were built into offices.

The Guaranty stands as the pinnacle of Sullivan's forward-thinking designs. His uniquely American architecture style greatly influenced the young Frank Lloyd Wright, who once worked for Adler and Sullivan.

n innovative architect often called "Father of Modernism" or "Father of Skyscrapers," Louis Sullivan pioneered the development of steel-frame architecture, which allowed for constructing large buildings to accommodate the growing residential and work needs in cities with limited ground space.

The building was renamed the Prudential Building in 1898 to acknowledge the financing provided by the Prudential Insurance Company. Both names adorn the principal entrances to the building.

The building was added to the National Register of Historic Places in 1973. After many years of decline and a fire in 1974, the Guaranty Building was able to avoid calls for demolition and has undergone a series of restorations to again take its place as one of Buffalo's premier office buildings.

PRUDENTIAL

786

Millionaires' Row

Nine elegant 19th-century mansions on Delaware Avenue, once home to the city's most conspicuously rich, are evidence of the Gilded Age grandeur found along Buffalo's "Millionaires' Row". These stunning examples of turn-of-the-century extravagance are of such astonishing size and opulence that they are used today as schools and offices for major corporations and not-for-profit organizations such as the American Red Cross. During Buffalo's heyday, more millionaires lived here in the Queen City than in any other city in the United States.

Opposite: The Clement House was built for Stephen M. Clement, president of Marine Bank, and his wife Carolyn, by Buffalo architects Green & Wicks. It was donated to the American Red Cross.

Top row left to right: The Grace Millard Knox Mansion • The George Brewster Mathews Mansion • Williams-Pratt House

Bottom row left to right: The Richmond-Lockwood Mansion • Williams-Butler House • The Charles W. Goodyear House

PITCO
Tri-Fri
MILLIE'S
419-453-3043
FINALLY A CUP DESIGNED FOR
DIPPING CHICKEN
WINGS!
NATIONAL BUFFALO
WING FESTIVAL
I STOPPED DIPPING THE TIP
(OF MY WINGS)
AT THE
BUFFALO WING
FESTIVAL
@CHICKEN_DIPPIN
RECYCLE
TRASH

Fairs & Festivals

*"If it's a weekend during the summer,
there's a festival to enjoy."*

– Just ask anyone

Whether it's celebrating a once-discarded chicken part, removing the ice boom, or attending a parade on the coldest day in March, here in Western New York, we aren't fussy about what excuse we use to throw a party for 100,000 of our closest friends.

We have festivals for corn, beer, canals, gardens, chalk, peaches, sexual orientation, pumpkins, and more beer. If you're Greek, Irish, German, Scottish, Puerto Rican, Italian, African-American, or any one of a dozen other nationalities, you've got your own festival. We have an art festival that lines the street to kick off the summer and an art festival that lines the street to bring it to a close.

We've even stated the obvious and defined music as art and throw a festival for that.

On the Monday following Easter, the people of Buffalo celebrate Dyngus Day, an odd Polish courting ritual. This massive party on the city's East Side is so much a part of our cultural DNA that it's included as an official holiday in city labor contracts.

In short, we love everything that makes living in Western New York amazing and are constantly searching to find inventive ways to enjoy them all to their fullest.

Left to Right: a Delicious sundae at the Niagara Peach Festival • Buffalo Pride Parade • Dyngus Day- A day of squirt guns, pussy willows, beer, polkas, festive costumes, and more beer. • One of dozens of Oktoberfest celebrations in WNY.

Opposite: THE NATIONAL BUFFALO WING FESTIVAL has become the "Super Bowl" of the chicken wing industry for restaurants, wing lovers, and even competitive eaters. While the rest of the world eats "Buffalo wings," here in our city, we eat "chicken wings" because we know that a buffalo is a furry, wingless mammal. First held in 2002, the festival serves more than half a million wings to as many as 90,000 attendees.

SHARE YOUR PLATE!
SMILE SUMMER
EAT DRINK LOCAL
City of Buffalo Recycles

Taking it to the streets

On weekends in Western New York, we flood the streets–not with water but with smiling people. Whether it's an ethnic, food, music, or arts festival, these flowing rivers of our citizenry showcase our neighborhood and the best of our cuisine, talent, and wares.

Italian-Heritage and Food Festival (Opposite)
Held in North Buffalo's Little Italy district, the Italian- Heritage and Food Festival was first celebrated on Hertel Avenue in 1988 and has grown to be the nation's second-largest Italian street festival. More than 600,000 people visit the four-day event each year to take in the sights, sounds, food, and culture that make the Italian-American experience so very special.

Allentown Art Festival (Above)
The Allentown Art Festival takes place in Buffalo's Allentown Historic Preservation District. Tens of thousands of art patrons visit the festival to enjoy the beauty of Buffalo's weather during the second weekend in June, the charm and uniqueness of the Allentown area, and the quality of the art and crafts presented by the over 400 juried exhibitors.

Since its modest beginnings in 1958, the Allentown Art Festival has become Buffalo's urban rite and a symbol for the enduring character of this re-emerging rust belt region. As a result, it has earned an important place in Buffalo's cultural and social life and a national reputation for excellence.

Erie County Fair

The Erie County Fair and Exposition is held in Hamburg every August. This is the third- largest county fair in the country, with an average attendance hovering around one million people.

From racing pigs, Chinese acrobats, and tractor pulls, to championship livestock, multiple concert stages, and a long list of everything possible to deep fry, the fair has something to amuse and delight the whole family.

Led by its first president, Dr. Cyrenius Chapin (more commonly known for his contribution in the War of 1812), the Agricultural Society was established in 1819. Then called the Niagara County Horticultural Society, it held its first fair in 1820 on what is now the site of HarborPlace and Canalside. One year later, Niagara County split into Erie and Niagara Counties, and so did the agricultural society. What began as a one-day event held in the fall has grown to become an 12-day event held each August. It has been held every year since 1841 with the exception of 1943, which was canceled because of World War II.

We love a parade

Other cities merely have parades. We throw linear parties with moving live music for thousands of our friends. And it doesn't take much of an excuse to throw one.

We march for African-American heritage, organized labor, veterans, sexual orientation, carnivals, Independence Day, a handful of ethnic festivals, and even a parade in the middle of our county fair. Some parades have floats that throw candy to the crowd, while others have crowds that soak the participants with squirt guns. And after a long Buffalo winter, we have so much pent-up Irish energy that it takes two parades to get it out of our system for another year.

"While some see our 'Old Neighborhood' St. Patrick's Day parade in the Old First Ward as people lining the streets to see the bands and the floats, I see the energy and spirit of a tightly-knit neighborhood brimming with pride."

Margaret "Peg" Overdorf
Executive Director
Valley Community Association

Opposite: Zuleika Grotto, a charitable organization dedicated to promoting friendship and fun amongst Master Freemasons, shown here marching in their signature outrageous outfits in the annual Fourth of July parade in Lancaster, N.Y.

Right: A tip of the hat from a St. Patrick's Day Parade reveler. Each year, thousands of people flock to downtown Buffalo to enjoy the Parade. It was first held on March 17, 1913, when a group of 5,000 Buffalo's Irish immigrants marched from the Elk Street Market Terminal to Euclid Place and back in sub-zero temperatures. However, the Parade was postponed in 1997 when more than 18 inches of snow fell, and wind chills of 30 below threatened frostbite.

UB

A College Town

A wide range of life-changing learning experiences and true affordability in an amazing city.

Unlike many college towns centralized around a single school, Buffalo is many college towns packed into an amazing and affordable city. The Western New York region is home to 15 four-year colleges and universities and 20 two-year colleges. With over 116,000 students enrolled, our colleges and universities graduate more than 27,000 students each year.

There is a fantastic variety of schools here specializing in a wide array of different fields. For example, UB has recently expanded its medical school, NCCC has an incredible culinary program, Buffalo State is well known for preparing future teachers, and the community colleges offer hundreds of career education possibilities.

Left to Right: Rockwell Hall at Buffalo State College • "Old Main" at Canisius College. Canisius is a private college in Buffalo, NY, and a premier Jesuit, Catholic University. • SUNY Erie downtown campus. With three campus locations, ECC offers more than 90 degree and certificate options.
• Niagara University Chapel. For more than 150 years. Niagara University has been educating students in the Catholic and Vincentian traditions. This tradition emphasizes ethics, lifelong learning, and service to others.
Opposite: Hayes Hall on UB's South Campus. A flagship institution in the State University of New York system, UB is the largest campus in the 64-campus SUNY system.

Waterfront

"We live in one of the most extraordinary places on earth. We're on the edge of one-fifth of the earth's surface fresh water."

Lawrence Brooks – Environmentalist/Author

As a city and as a region, we are completely inseparable from our water. It's an embarrasment of wealth that is our connection to our past, present, and future.

We depend on this water for our power, recreation, industry, and agriculture. It has separated us in war. and it's what binds us in peace.For good and for bad our water dictates our weather.

Our waterfront is an important part of our identity to the world, by reflecting its radiant beauty. Where our water becomes a thundering cataract, it's visited by millions.

In short, our water is the glue that binds us together.

This fluid connection, however, is only a magnificent illusion. The same water we gaze out upon today isn't the same water we'll see tomorrow. While seemingly abundant and permanent, our glue is constantly racing away at the staggering rate of 750,000 gallons per minute.

This is a chapter to celebrate its journey, and an invitation to fully enjoy and protect its wonder..

Left to Right: Explore the waterfront with a single or tandem water bike. They can be rented on the Boardwalk at Canalside. • Whether you call it a boat, a bike, or a floating pedal pub, Buffalo Cycleboats are an unforgettable experience! • Times Beach Nature Preserve is a unique place that attracts more birds and more varieties of birds than almost any place in the Great Lakes. Show here is a Great Egret. • The iconic 1833 Buffalo Lighthouse at the main entrance to Buffalo Harbor was first lit in 1833 and served until 1914.
Opposite: The inner harbor as seen from the gantry crane operator during the construction of Harborside © Photo by Paul "the Craneman" Hopkins

CARICATURES
CARTOONS!
OBX

Canalside

Situated on 21 historic acres of Buffalo's inner harbor, Canalside is a growing regional destination and entertainment district. It has fast become the go-to place for residents and tourists alike, with more than 1,000 yearly events and nearly 1 million annual visitors and growing.

With roots dating back to 1825, Canalside takes its name from its storied past when the Erie Canal Harbor was the western terminus of the Erie Canal and was veritably the gateway to the West. Today it is the gateway to Buffalo's future, blending its historic underpinnings with a considerable upswing in private and public development.

As poignant reminders of its glorious past, there are many original elements at Canalside, including the refurbished "Commercial Slip," "Central Wharf," "Whipple Truss" footbridge, cobblestone streets, and the excavated foundations of several canal-era buildings. Re-watered canals now serve as a family playground with paddleboats in summer, roller skating in the Fall, and ice skating in winter.

Whether you are coming for an event or merely to hang out for fun, Canalside has a packed calendar of options for kids and families, fitness enthusiasts, music lovers, history buffs, festival-goers, and more.

Explore the waterfront with a Blue Bike, water bike, or kayak rental. Step back in time on the Spirit of Buffalo, a History Tour Boat ride, or a Canalside walking tour. Shop at the Saturday Artisan Market, play in the giant sandbox, take an art class, or watch a movie.

Eat, drink and be merry with a bite from The Dish or a brew from the Beer and Wine Garden.

You can get your blood pumping with outdoor fitness classes, such as Zumba, Power Yoga, Exercise Like the Animals, and Tai Chi, or just relax on the big, colorful, Adirondack chairs and read a book and enjoy the sunset.

Opposite: A typical weekend crowd enjoying the many vendors at Canalside.

Right: Kayaks and Waterbikes are popular personal watercraft rentals.

Re-watered Canal

Canalside is a magical place for young and formerly young kids filled with dozens of ways to capture their imaginations. It's buzzing with tons of children's programming, history tours, and outdoor activities.

(Opposite:) You can paddle your way through Buffalo's history, where shallow canals have been restored to how they were in 1825. Adult pedal boats and children's paddle boats, manufactured right here in Western New York, are available for hourly rental. When the temperatures dip below freezing, Canalside, Buffalo's beloved summertime waterfront destination, magically transforms.

The Historic Replica Canals, where paddleboats once cruised, now become a winter wonderland on New York State's largest outdoor ice skating rink. During Buffalo's fourth season, this becomes the domain of ice skating, ice biking (invented here in Buffalo), curling, and ice bumper cars on 33,000 square feet of ice.

Ice Bumper Cars (Below:)
The newest way to enjoy the ice is to slip, slide and smash your ice bumper car with your friends and family.

Phillips Lytle LLP
there are
discounts
BLUE

Buffalo Heritage Carousel

The historic century-old De Angelis Menagerie Carousel's 34 hand-carved animals were built in 1924 at the Herschell-Spillman factory in North Tonawanda but then went into storage for 80 years. The hand-carved wooden animals, chariots, brass poles, complete with lively organ music, is a commanding presence that children can now enjoy for generations to come. A computer now powers the music scrolls played by an antique Wurlitzer Carousel Band Organ.

The solar-powered carousel, which was meticulously restored for four years, will be located on the Canalside boardwalk near Clinton's Dish inside a glass-enclosed roundhouse. Its sights and sounds are a grand celebration of both Buffalo's industrial history and our ongoing work to revive and transform Buffalo's Waterfront.

The eco-friendly Tesla solar panels on the Buffalo Heritage Carousel are a modern chapter to the history of carousel manufacturing in Western New York. It underscores our legacy of leadership in the use of renewable energy that began in 1901 with the transmission of hydro-electric power from Niagara Falls to Buffalo.

A whirling ride on the carousel may only be three minutes long but can leave memories to last a lifetime.

BUFFALO
SAL

The Longshed Building

New at the northern end of the Central Wharf is the Longshed building; a two-story, gabled-roof wood structure reflects the site's history. It incorporates elements from the Joy and Webster Storehouse located on the site in the early 1800s.

The approximately 4,400-square-foot Longshed includes a main floor that stretches the building's length, a smaller mezzanine level, public bathrooms, roll-up entry doors, and an exterior porch that overlooks the Canalside lawn.

Initially, the building will be used by staff and volunteers from the Buffalo Maritime Center to construct a replica of the 1825 Seneca Chief packet boat, which transported Governor DeWitt Clinton from Buffalo to New York City to mark the official opening of the Erie Canal.

The packet boat project is expected to take about three years to complete. During that time, the public will be able to watch the boat being built and even volunteer to join the construction crew!Once completed, the packet boat will be relocated to the Commercial Slip, where the Buffalo Maritime Center will make it available to tourists interested in learning more about the region's past. The boat will also tour other sections of the Erie Canal system to promote Buffalo and its history.

Explore & More

The Ralph C. Wilson, Jr. Children's Museum

Promoted as "Where fun and learning play together," Explore & More-The Ralph C. Wilson, Jr. Children's Museum is a 43,000 sq. ft, world-class children's museum that celebrates the power of child-led play.

Tucked between Canalside's replica canals and bridges, the museum has become a year-round must-see destination for anyone with children. There are four floors of fun with seven different play zones to explore, featuring thoughtfully crafted exhibits. They are designed to help children develop a deeper sense of our world, our community, and their place in it. Learning seamlessly happens here in a fun and engaging way for children and adults alike.

The museum amplifies our sense of place by showcasing Buffalo's history, waterways, sports teams, diversity, and invention contributions. Children can also learn how to grow plants, cook a meal, and be creative in the art studio.

Explore & More is a place where learning feels like playing, where "Do not touch" becomes "Try it out". And where there's always a reason to come back for more.

ARRIOTT
LOW BRIDGE CAFE
explore &more

FLIP-ER'

Inner Harbor

Once just a river lined with wharves and grain elevators comprising the world's largest trans-shipment point of grain, this is now the focal point of recreational waterfront activity. And the piers have become home to battleships, tour boats, and recreational watercraft from kayaks and water bikes, to a line of sailboat slips as far as the eye can see.

Opposite:
Power and sailboats raft several deep, creating a temporary party platform for revelry among the boating community.

Left:
Queen City Bike Ferry is a convenient link for non-motorized vehicles between the Commercial Slip at Canalside and the Bike Ferry Landing on the Outer Harbor. This inexpensive 600-foot passage across the Buffalo River provides easy walking and bike access to points on the Outer Harbor.

Below:
The grain elevators now magically transform at night to spectacular canvasses for a blaze of colored light imagery. In 1901 the city of Buffalo, New York hosted the Pan American Exposition, which featured dazzling displays of electricity, inspiring awe in its visitors and earning it the nickname the "City of Light". The Connecting Terminal Grain Elevator, easily seen from the boardwalk at Canalside, is the canvas for this breathtaking light show. It beautifully projects our four seasons as though being viewed through the lens of a kaleidoscope. © Photo by Eileen Elibol

Erie Basin Harbor

It's easy to forget that the Erie Basin Marina, one of the most popular places on the Buffalo waterfront, was once just a breakwater and commercial slip at the mouth of the Buffalo River at Lake Erie designed to lessen the impact of storm surges.

Previously just a breakwater not even connected to the mainland, in 1970-1973, a major lakefront improvement project constructed the road, walkways, marina, tower, and buildings. Hidden to all but birds, airline pilots, and people viewing it from the City Hall observation deck is the fact that the marina was designed in the shape of a buffalo.

Today Erie Basin Marina is so much more than a giant parking lot for boats. It is actually a neighborhood, complete with offices, condos, and restaurants.

Visitors come to watch sailboats skim gracefully past the historic lighthouse while surrounded by fabulous professionally groomed gardens. They can build an appetite as they scale the 83 steps of the Outlook Tower for the city's best panoramic views and then enjoy comfort food, ice cream, and occasionally good Karaoke at The Hatch restaurant. Of course, many just come for their daily stroll or to sit and observe the fantastic sunsets that glimmer across the lake.

Buffalo and Erie County Naval and Military Park

Adjacent to Buffalo's Canalside is the Buffalo and Erie County Naval & Military Park, the largest inland naval and military museum park displays in the country. Public tours to the park give visitors the opportunity to view several decommissioned U.S. Naval vessels that include the Cleveland-class guided-missile cruiser U.S.S. Little Rock, the Fletcher-class destroyer U.S.S. The Sullivans, and the Gato Class submarine U.S.S. Croaker.

"Western New Yorkers have participated in every war our country has fought in, with many paying the ultimate price so we can enjoy our freedom. After returning home, these veterans have greatly contributed to our community and have made Western New York the vibrant area we know and love."

–Colonel Patrick Cunningham
Former Executive Director
Buffalo and Erie County Naval & Military Park

Opposite: Built just after the U.S. entry into World War II, U.S.S. Croaker was sent to the Pacific to wage a war of attrition against Japan's merchant marine and Navy. © Photo by Laura Donnelly

Right: The Fletcher-class destroyer U.S.S. The Sullivans was launched in 1943 and decommissioned in 1965. She is named for the five Sullivan brothers who lost their lives in the battle of the Solomon Islands when their ship sank.

246

BUFFALO RIVER

The Buffalo River, once most noted for its ability to catch fire, thanks to the dedication of groups like Buffalo Niagara Riverkeeper is now a bustling waterway alive with recreational boaters. It has rapidly transformed in recent decades from an industrial river to a natural landscape. Wildlife and vegetation have quickly returned to the river's banks as industry has left, and it creates a poignant counterpoint to the towering concrete grain elevators.

Whether by tour boat or by kayak, the best way to appreciate Buffalo's industrial heritage and the nation's largest collection of standing grain elevators is from the water. You'll be traveling along the waterway that made Buffalo the largest grain port in the world and one of the biggest and wealthiest cities in its day.

The Buffalo River is home to the historic Buffalo Lighthouse, Buffalo and Erie County Naval & Military Park, Canalside, RiverWorks, Silo City, Riverfest, and Mutual Riverfront Park, Buffalo Scholastic Rowing, Elevator Alley, and more.

Left: Kayak launch at Mutual Riverfront Park

Below: Buffalo Scholastic Rowing is keeping alive the long-standing tradition of competitive rowing on the Buffalo River

Opposite: Buffalo River History Tours boat nearing the Michigan Avenue bridge.

(716) 796-4556
BUFFALO RIVER HISTORY TOURS
RIVER QUEEN
BUFFALO RIVER HISTORY TOURS

14921

Outer Harbor

There's a newly reborn landscape on Buffalo's Lake Erie shoreline. Once seen as barren and isolated, the Outer Harbor is now both accessible and the site of much of what makes summer fun. The advent of concerts, festivals, miles of bike trails, a new state park, kayak launch sites, and awe-inspiring nature and scenery have pumped new life into the stretch of land between the historic 1833 Lighthouse and Gallagher Beach.

The Queen City Bike Ferry that connects Canalside with the north end of the Outer Harbor and the Ohio Street bike path opening are both a huge part of this revival. From the bike ferry, whose ride for a mere dollar across the inner harbor is enjoyable in its own right, and there's a world of wonder within easy walking or biking distance.

A path that parallels the Buffalo Coast Guard Base will take you right to the foot of the Historic 1833 Lighthouse. Next door. Experience the sights and sounds of the natural world as you walk the paths and boardwalks at Times Beach Nature Preserve.

Right: A stunning sunset from the pier at Gallagher Beach
Below: Historic 1833 Lighthouse
Opposite: Personal watercraft at Gallagher Beach.

On the water

There is no better view of our amazing waterfront than actually being on the water. Whether it is on the Maid of the Mist seeing a natural wonder of the world from the bottom up; or touring our river and lakes on the Miss Buffalo, Grand Lady, Spirit of Buffalo, and Moondance Cat, Western New York never looks better than when you are surrounded by water with the sun in your face and the wind in your hair.

Moondance Cat *(Right)*
Now enjoying more than 40 years in operation, Moondance Cat is a 65-passenger elite sailing Catamaran whose parallel hulls are joined by a "party" deck that supports a full bar and plenty of room for mingling.

Miss Buffalo II *(below)*
Come aboard Miss Buffalo II for daily sightseeing cruises and incredible sunsets and evening views of the city.

Spirit of Buffalo *(Opposite)*
Enjoy the skyline and the colorful sunsets over Lake Erie as you sail back in time aboard the Spirit of Buffalo. You'll truly discover the feel of traditional sailing on this classic 73-foot topsail schooner. You'll be invited to join the crew and hoist its distinctive red sails, or you can sit back, relax, and see the city in a new way.

Joy!

One of our greatest commodities

While "joy" is easily defined, there are very few places on earth where you have so many ways to achieve it.

Here in Western New York, we share the pleasure of enjoying some of the best skiing, fishing, golfing, and boating in the Northeast. Whether it's served on a table between four walls, or through a window over four wheels, we've got great eats. And there are equally great brews to wash it down.

Culture in this region is hard to miss and easy to enjoy. We've got world-class architecture, world-class galleries, a world-class symphony orchestra, and some of the most incredibly talented people in the galaxy.

Because we have four actual seasons, we can get sand in our shoes, jump in a giant pile of leaves, and make snow angels, all in the same year.

There's a multitude of places and events to connect with hundreds of your friends and "not yet friends," and solitude always within reach in our fabulous parks.

Most of all, this is a city with a pulse that can make your smile grow wider with every beat. We live amid sixty canoes piled on a pole, Monty the Therapy Dog, a cemetery with a life-size black marble couch and loveseat, the world's largest six-pack, a brain museum, tailgating with Pinto Kenny, a little girl with a shark's head, and a guy who perpetually blows bubbles out his street corner window.

Western New York truly is a joyous place to live, work, and play.

Opposite: A band entertains a gathering of neighbors and friends at Porchfest.
(Left to right:) A herd of bikers pedaling to end cancer at the annual Ride for Roswell. • Take a tiki boat cruise on inner harbor while sipping on a Hawaiian cocktail. • Enjoy the fabulous sunsets as they stretch across the waters at Wendt Beach • Floating at the tip of Kelly Island, the World's largest rubber duck visited Canalside as part of the Buffalo Maritime Festival.

THE JOY OF ART IS EVERYWHERE

While we have more than our fair share of galleries, large and small, our exuberance for art can't be held in by walls. Hand-painted murals decorate our urban walls, sculptures and statuary dot our street corners and line our expressways, and our airport and transit stations are alive with creative work.

Opposite:
Renowned Brazilian muralist Eduardo Kobra's rendering of Twain and longtime friend John Lewis along Hertel Avenue is part of the Albright-Knox Art Gallery's Public Art initiative.

Twain made the acquaintance of John T. Lewis in the event of Lewis' heroic actions stopping a runaway horse and buggy carrying Twain's sister-in-law and her daughter from near-certain death. Historians have speculated Lewis was the inspiration for "Jim" in Twain's classic novel Huckleberry Finn. Lewis and Twain are buried next to each other in Elmira, New York.

This mural is one of the hundreds that have recently appeared on city walls helping to make Buffalo even more visually exciting.

Right:
On one of the bridges crossing the re-watered canals, Shark Girl patiently sits in her best dress, hands folded, and legs daintily crossed. This lonely half-shark, half-girl is waiting for a companion to come join her on her boulder. It's a tantalizing invitation to initiate a friendship and perhaps have your picture taken with her.

:

THE AFRICAN AMERICAN CULTURAL CENTER INC
PINE GRILL JAZZ REUNION

Tuesday in the Park concert at Artpark © Photo by Aaron Bobeck

SHARING MUSIC WITH SEVERAL THOUSAND OF OUR CLOSEST FRIENDS

Pine Grill Reunion *(Left:)*
The Pine Grill Jazz Reunion, held annually on the first two Sundays in August in Martin Luther King, Jr. Park, is one of the city's premier musical experiences. The free concerts celebrate Buffalo's rich jazz legacy. During the 1950s and 1960s, the Pine Grill nightclub on Jefferson Avenue near East Ferry Street was a hot stop on the national jazz circuit. Jazz greats like Miles Davis, Dizzy Gillespie, and Billie Holiday graced its stage. Although the club was closed and demolished in the mid-1980s, the legend of this jazz treasure lives on through these concerts.

Artpark *(Above)*
Each summer, Artpark presents an exciting variety of concerts, theater performances, and Broadway musicals in the 2400-seat Mainstage Theater and adjacent seating lawn. In addition, Artpark's outdoor amphitheater is home to the popular "Tuesday in the Park" and the "Coors Light Wednesdays" summer concert series. Artpark also offers families free art activities, unique camps for children, and visual arts experiences.

Where Buffalo Graze

While we have dozens of excellent fine dining restaurants, with exceptionally talented young chefs serving everything from farm to table to innovative ethnic fare, we always tend to gravitate back to our blue-collar pub food roots.

We're hooked on our regional classics like chicken wings, char-grilled Ted's hot dogs, beef on weck, fish fry, and anything else that pairs well with an ice-cold brew and a football game.

Our hometown is the birthplace of many foods we love and ground zero for culinary treasures like Cheerios, Sahlen's Hot Dogs, Weber's Mustard, Galbani Cheese, and Bison Chip Dip.

Right: The official greeter at the world-famous Anchor Bar, said to be the origin of the Buffalo chicken wing. She works for tips.

Below: Charlie the Butcher is a staple of Western New York's food scene for decades, serving Buffalo's iconic Beef on Weck and other fresh carved sandwiches.

Opposite: In the summer of 2010, Lloyd's hit the Buffalo streets, developing the first of a growing food truck scene and proving that great food is not the sole domain of brick-and-mortar restaurants. Today there are enough fantastic local food trucks to create their own traffic jam.

ORDER
LL YD TACO TRUCKS
@WHERESLLOYD

Retail Therapy

From large malls and quaint antique shops, to Elmwood boutiques and cultural gift shops, Western New York has seemingly endless ways to enjoy the shopping experience. It feels good to put your money where your heart is. Now more than ever, it is important for us to stand together and support each other – which means that each of us has to do our part to keep local businesses open, and our neighbors safe and employed.

Right:
With over 75,000 different items spread out over two floors in four connected buildings, Vidler's in East Aurora is arguably the largest 5 & 10 in the world. Owned and operated by the Vidler family since its opening in 1930, this isn't just shopping; it's an adventure. It's easy to wander their squeaky wooden floors intoxicated by the overflowing abundance of nostalgia and unique products for hours.

Opposite:
Since 1888, the Broadway Market has celebrated our city's food, people, and enduring legacy. The sounds and smells of this old-world public market are provided by family-owned businesses that have passed from generation to generation and are responsible for some of Buffalo's best-loved foods.

Although it's open year-round, the Broadway Market best known as a holiday tradition. For many, it is an annual pre-Easter pilgrimage to wade through the crowds to buy their pierogi, a butter lamb, pussy willows, and any confection imaginable dipped in chocolate.

BUTTER LAMBS
FRESH CHICKEN
WIXSON'S
Orange Blossom

Tim Hortons
GEICO
BILLS

"Top shelf, where momma hides the cookies."

–John Richard "Rick" Jeanneret
Play-by-play announcer for the Buffalo Sabres

If sports is your religion, then Buffalo is your church. It's hard to overestimate just how passionate Western New Yorkers are about their sports. We're home to two major league sports teams, the Buffalo Sabres and the Buffalo Bills, as well as several minor sports teams, including the Buffalo Bisons, Buffalo Bandits indoor lacrosse, and FC Buffalo soccer. The Buffalo Niagara region also offers a diverse variety of college and university athletic programs.

Our fan loyalty is legendary. As a city not known for our fair weather, we're also not known for having fair weather fans. Despite many crushing and sometimes controversial defeats such as "Wide Right", "No Goal", and the "Music City Miracle," our resilient spirit has never allowed it to define us as fans. Our capacity crowds consistently show up in full colors and always leave a little bit hoarse from cheering on our teams. Some of us even include being the 12th man on our résumés.

Entertainment Magnets

Larkinville *(Left)*

Self-described as "Whimsy Amongst the Warehouses," this former site of Buffalo's famed Larkin Soap Company is now one of the hippest places in town. Centered around Seneca Street, southeast of downtown Buffalo, this revitalized industrial area has been spectacularly transformed into a thriving hub of restaurants, microbreweries, and other businesses.

The epicenter of Larkinville is Larkin Square, which opened in 2012. Its eclectic mix of playful architecture provides the perfect backdrop to gather for live music, food, and fun.

Buffalo RiverWorks *(Opposite)*

One of the city's premier entertainment destinations is a highly innovative adaptive reuse of Buffalo's historic grain elevators on the site of the old GLF Mills. Beneath the distinctive six-pack of silos on the banks of the Buffalo River is a 60,000-foot indoor event center featuring multiple bars and restaurants, a 5,000-person concert venue, a 1,500-person banquet facility, and space for trade shows, corporate events, and conventions.

The water-accessible facility has two hockey rinks, a fully functioning brewery, and houses the world's first permanent, purpose-built, flat-track roller derby track.

© Photo by Joe Cascio

Labatt
Blue
IMPORTED
NO PRESERVATIVES
RIVER QUEEN
Buffalo, NY

A Brilliant Future

"Our vision is to attract the best and the brightest. A combination of world-class facilities, and a reinvigorated community that people are excited to be a part of, will allow us to do just that."

– Matt Enstice, President & CEO
Buffalo Niagara Medical Campus

While we still have a ways to go as a city and a region, there is a noticeable sea change taking place here. There's a noticeable new spring in our walk and twinkle in our eye knowing that our trajectory is changing toward the positive.

The signs are everywhere. Our skyline is quickly morphing as construction cranes dot the horizon. High technology manufacturing is sprouting up where "rust belt" steel plants once stood. The Buffalo Niagara Medical Campus is now home to the UB Medical School and John R. Oishei Children's Hospital. 43 North has been a fantastic catalyst for entrepreneurial innovation. Our youth is beginning to return or deciding not to leave at all. And the Waterfront is bustling at a rate few thought was possible. And that's not to mention that the Buffalo Bills are so red hot we've informally renamed Allentown - Allen Town.

Our foot is firmly on the gas pedal, and there is a palpable excitement about what is around the next corner. Once again, we're "Talkin' Proud" because there truly is so much to love.

(Left to Right:) Some of the most innovative medicine in the country – and the world – is being performed right here in Buffalo, at the Gates Vascular Institute. • The DL&W Terminal is proposed to become a major destination again at the foot of Main Street and transforming this massive and historic building into a first-class recreational, commercial, and economic development site. • Our AFC East Champion Buffalo Bills have relit the torch inside their already rabid fan base with dreams of a Superbowl win feeling closer. • The $160 million Albright Knox AK360 expansion project will add another 30,000 square feet to its campus.

(Opposite:) Things are looking up. © Photo by Paul "the Craneman" Hopkins

This portrait of the author was part of *Artists Seen: Photographs of Artists in the 21st Century*, an ongoing project by photographer David Moog in partnership with the Burchfield Penney Art Center. This is the Center's tribute to every artist who works to realize their personal vision.

About the Author

In 2008 with the release of my first Buffalo pictorial book, *The Fine Art of Capturing Buffalo*, I was then described as "an artist, an educator, a passionate community activist, a proud husband and father, and a man seldom separated from his camera."

Twenty-two books later, other than the city visually exploding with great new things, nothing has changed.

Acknowledgements

I am deeply honored to be part of a book that includes many of the region's top photographers. They have graciously allowed the use of their images in support of community initiatives.

Jackie Albarella
Aaron Bobeck
Mark Brice, Buffalo Aerial Pictures
Joe Cascio
Chautauqua Institution
Mark Dellas
Laura Donnelly
Eileen Elibol
Paul "the Craneman" Hopkins
Alan Kotok
David Moog
Nickel City Studio

www.ingramcontent.com/pod-product-compliance
Lightning Source LLC
LaVergne TN
LVHW072327100826
845147LV00004B/657

* 9 7 8 1 9 5 6 6 8 8 0 3 0 *